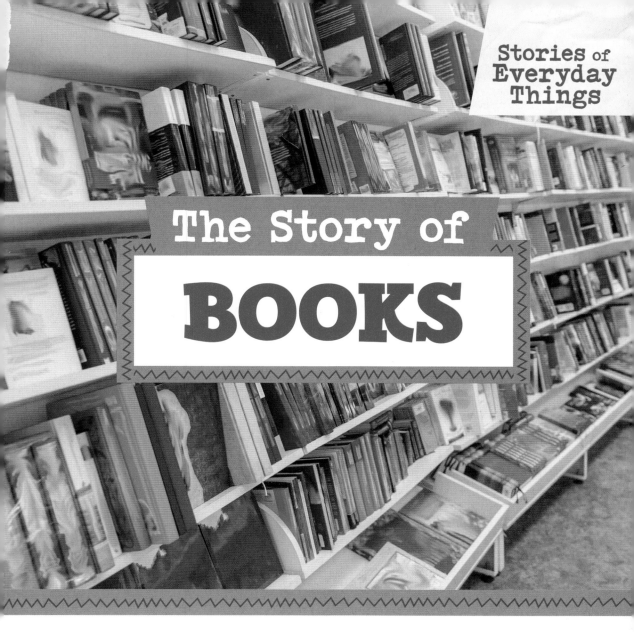

Stories of Everyday Things

The Story of BOOKS

by Mae Respicio

PEBBLE
a capstone imprint

T0020147

Published by Pebble, an imprint of Capstone
1710 Roe Crest Drive, North Mankato, Minnesota 56003
capstonepub.com

Library of Congress Cataloging-in-Publication Data
is available on the Library of Congress website.
ISBN: 9780756577483 (hardcover)
ISBN: 9780756577759 (paperback)
ISBN: 9780756577544 (ebook PDF)

Summary: Who invented books? What materials are
used to make a book? How do books make it onto shelves
around the world? These questions and many more will be
answered in this book about books.

Editorial Credits
Editor: Christianne Jones; Designer: Jaime Willems;
Media Researcher: Rebekah Hubstenberger; Production
Specialist: Whitney Schaefer

Image Credits
Alamy: Classic Image, 13; Getty Images: China Photos, 11,
Grafissimo, 16, Hulton Archive, 10, iStock/industryview,
21, JEAN-FRANCOIS MONIER/AFP, 20, kupicoo, 27, LLUIS
GENE/AFP, 25, mikroman6, 15, pictafolio, 5; Shutterstock:
Amero, Cover (right), Baloncici, 22, belov1409, Cover
(middle left), Dmytro Zinkevych, Back Cover, George Rudy,
1, jannoon028, 29, Marco Ossino, 7, Monkey Business
Images, 4, New Africa, Cover (bottom left, top right), Olga
Razryadova, Cover (top middle), Vtmila, Cover (top left),
zefart, 19, 23; The Metropolitan Museum of Art: Rogers
Fund, 1930, 9

Design Elements
Shutterstock: Luria, Pooretat moonsana

Printed and bound in China. PO 5593

Table of Contents

Words in bold appear in the glossary.

History of Books

Books help us learn. They entertain us. They spark our imagination. Books are for everyone!

Books come in different forms. They can be printed, **electronic**, and **audio**. There are more than 150 million titles in the world today!

But books have been a part of our lives since ancient times. Long ago, people wrote stories on stone slabs and bark. The ancient Egyptians wrote on many things. They used clay, stone, and bone.

They also wrote on material from a plant called **papyrus**. Egyptians wove the plant stems together. Then they pounded them flat. This made a page.

Strips and rolled sheets from the stems of papyrus

They used pens to write on each page. But they didn't use pens like you use. Their pens were made from **reeds**. Then pages were glued together to form a long scroll. A scroll is a long book that is rolled up.

A scroll is one of the first types of books. The longest Egyptian scroll ever found stretched more than 133 feet (40 meters) long! That's as long as the Statue of Liberty is tall.

After the scroll came the codex. This was what ancient Romans called their book. A codex was made of materials such as papyrus and **parchment**. They bound the pages together. A codex looked similar to what a book looks like now.

Part of an ancient Egyptian scroll on papyrus

At first, people made books. Each page was written by hand. It took a very long time. What changed this? The woodblock.

In 868 CE, Chinese craftsmen carved pictures and words into a woodblock with knives. Each block had a full page of words and pictures on it. They put ink on the blocks. Then they pressed them onto paper.

The paper they used was made from many materials. These included **hemp**, bark, mulberries, and even fish nets. The materials formed **pulp**. The pulp was pressed and dried to make a page.

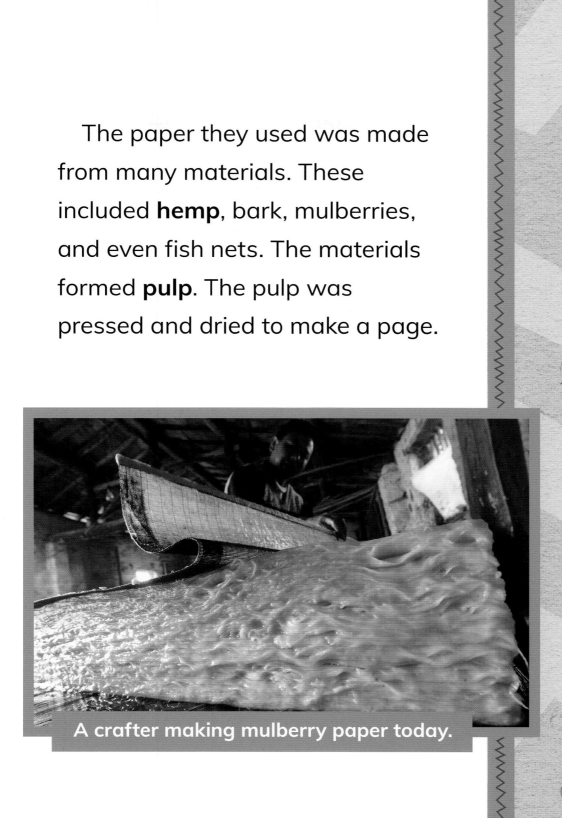

A crafter making mulberry paper today.

The Power of Print

Around 1000, movable type was invented in China. Each letter was on a different piece of block. The letters could be moved around. They could be used over and over.

The original pieces were made with baked clay. They broke easily. Soon after, wooden movable type was used. It was stronger. Later, the pieces were made with metal. Metal was heavy. But it lasted the longest.

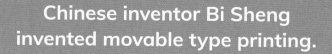

Chinese inventor Bi Sheng invented movable type printing.

Movable type is considered the first printing technology. Later, people in Europe and Africa began to use movable type to make books.

Around 1440, one of the most important inventions for books came. What was it? The printing press! In Germany, Johannes Gutenberg made a mechanical device that put ink onto paper. Instead of using wood or clay, it used metal.

Gutenberg looks at a page from his press.

Incipit epistola sancti iheronimi ad
paulinum presbiterum de omnibus
diuine historie libris·capitulum primum.

Rater ambrosius
tua michi munus-
cula pferens·detulit
sit et suauissimas
lras·q a principio
amiciciaz·fide pba-
te iam fidei z veteris amicicie noua:
pferebant. Vera enim illa necessitudo est
z xpi glutino copulata·quam non vtili-
tas rei familiaris·non pntia tantum
corpoz·non subdola z palpans adulaco-
sed dei timor·et diuinaz scripturaru
studia conciliant. legim9 in veteribz
historijs·quosdam lustrasse puincias.
nouos adiisse pplos·maria trasisse
ut eos quos ex libris nouerant:cora
qq viderent. Sicut pitagoras memphi-
ticos vates·sic plato egiptum z architam
tarentinum·eandemq oram ytalie·que
quondam magna grecia dicebat:labo-
riosissime peragauit·et ut qui athenis
mgr erat·z poteus·cuiusqz doctrinas

Page from the Gutenberg Bible

16

The printing press made books quickly. It could make many at a time. Gutenberg printed lots of materials. In 1455, he printed the Bible. It was known as the Gutenberg Bible.

The printing press changed how books were made. It brought books to many people. It is how the book we know today was born.

How Books Are Made Today

Creating a story is a lot of work. It takes a full team of people, which can include authors, editors, illustrators, photo researchers, and more. Once the story is through the creative process, it can be printed.

Books are printed in large printing plants around the world. Printing presses can print thousands of pages at a time. It is done at high speeds. The presses can make books in different shapes and sizes.

Printing plate

To print a book, plates are used. Plates are large, thin sheets of metal. The book information is burned onto a printing plate. Then ink is rolled onto each plate. The ink transfers onto the paper that runs through the press.

Today, paper is made from plant fibers. It is a material that must be manufactured. Fibers are turned into a pulp and mixed with water. A machine flattens, dries, and cuts the paper into sheets or rolls.

Paper roll at a paper-making factory

Books are printed on those long rolls of paper. Machines cut them from large sheets into smaller ones. The pages are folded in half and sewn together. These bundles are called signatures.

Folded book pages

A book goes into a machine for cutting, trimming, and binding.

Is the book finished yet? Not quite! A binding machine glues the pages to the **spine** of the book's cover. However, the pages are still folded. A machine needs to trim the pages so you can open the book.

How Books Make it to Shelves

Readers can get books in many ways. They are **distributed** through stores, libraries, and online.

Usually stores buy printed books in batches from a wholesaler. Wholesalers buy a book from a **publisher**. They then have a supply of books to sell to libraries, bookstores, and other businesses. These places use the books for their own customers. A wholesaler keeps books in giant warehouses until they are ready to be shipped.

Worker in a book warehouse

Once books get delivered, they can be displayed on shelves. People can buy the books. They can check them out from libraries. At last, the books can be enjoyed.

Modern books have come a long way. People can read them on paper and electronically. They can listen to them on their devices or in their cars. No matter how we read our books, we learn from them. They're one of many everyday things used in our everyday lives.

Make a Mini Book

It takes a long time to make a book. However, you can easily make a mini book and become your own publisher!

What you need:

- paper (at least five sheets)
- scissors
- stapler
- pencil, pen, markers, or crayons

What you do:

1. Cut several sheets of letter-sized paper in half.

2. Stack them and fold them in half.

3. Staple along the crease.

4. Smooth out any wrinkles.

5. Write your own story. Be sure to include a title and your name. You can also include drawings or designs. Now you have a small book!

Glossary

audio (AW-dee-oh)—having to do with how sound is heard, recorded, and played back

distribute (diss-TRIB-yoot)—to deliver products to various places

electronic (i-lek-TRAH-nik)—relating to a device powered by electricity; computers, TVs, radios, and tablets are electronic

hemp (HEMP)—a tall Asian herb used for its tough fiber, seeds, and oil

papyrus (puh-PYE-ruhss)—a tall water plant that grows in northern Africa and southern Europe; a material that is written on can be made from the stems of this plant

parchment (PARCH-muhnt)—writing material made from animal skins

publisher (PUHB-lish-ur)—a company that produces and distributes a book or other printed material so that people can buy it

pulp (PUHLP)—a mixture of ground up materials and water

reed (REED)—a tall plant with hollow stems that grows in wetlands

spine (SPINE)—the part of a book to which the pages are attached

Read More

Barr, Catherine, and Steve Williams. *The Story of Inventions: A First Book About World-Changing Discoveries.* London, England: Frances Lincoln Children's Books, 2020.

Meister, Cari. *From Trees to Paper.* Mankato, MN: Amicus, 2020.

Toolen, Avery. From *Trees to Paper.* Minneapolis: Jump!, 2022.

Internet Sites

Curious Kids: How Are Books Made? kiowacountypress.net/content/curious-kids-how-are-books%C2%A0made

How Are Books Made Today?: A Visit to the Almanac Printer! almanac.com/how-are-books-made-today-visit-almanac-printer

Top 10 Facts About Books! funkidslive.com/learn/top-10-facts/top-10-facts-about-books

Index

About the Author

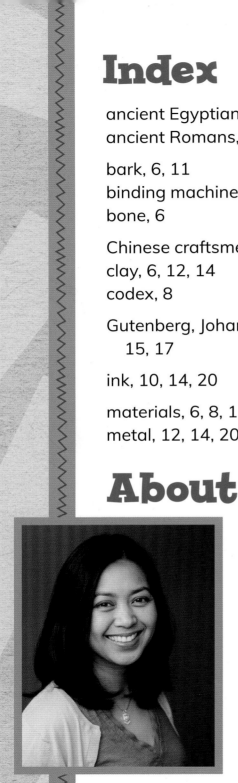

Mae Respicio is a nonfiction writer and middle grade author whose novel, *The House That Lou Built,* won an Asian/Pacific American Libraries Association Honor Award and was an NPR Best Book. Mae lives with her family in California and some of her favorite everyday things include books, beaches, and ube ice cream.